ODD ODES
FOR OLDIES

ODD ODES
FOR OLDIES

H ELEN I NGS

Illustrated by Hannah Purkiss

Library of Congress Control Number:		2016917262
ISBN:	Hardcover	978-1-5245-9507-4
	Softcover	978-1-5245-9506-7
	eBook	978-1-5245-9505-0

Print information available on the last page.

Rev. date: 03/15/2017

To order additional copies of this book, contact:
Xlibris
800-056-3182
www.Xlibrispublishing.co.uk
Orders@Xlibrispublishing.co.uk
746387

This little book of nonsense poems
is dedicated to the memory of Bill.
Special thanks to Sharon for all her help
and to Alison, Tina, June, Daphne, Barbara,
Pat, Sandra, Margaret and all my special
family. Thank you for all your patience
and for indulging me!

Contents

Wishful Thinking!

If only I could have my time again . . .
Then I'd be THIN!

I wouldn't have to diet all the time . . .
I'd just be THIN!

I'd sit there eating chocolates all night long . . .
And still be THIN!

I wouldn't have to keep a 'padlock' on . . .
THE COOKIE TIN!

I'd gorge all day on scrummy Fish and Chips . . .
And Apple Pie and Cream and Walnut Whips . . .
And none of it would end up on my hips . . .
'Cos I'd be THIN!

One Foot in the Grave!

'Let go!' said the Robin—'I saw it first!'
But the sparrow insisted, 'It's mine!'
So they pulled and they tugged on the poor centipede—
Till they very near broke his wee spine!

Then a wise old Thrush flew down from above—
Quite distressed by their squabbling and flapping.
He would hear from both sides and determine who's right—
If they only would stop all their scrapping!

And the Centipede smiled and lay very still,
So the birds would all think that he'd 'pegged' it!
Then, quick as a flash, when their backs were all turned—
He picked up his feet, and he legged it!

Capability Clown!

Come into my garden
If you've got the time to spare!
Take the weight from off your feet . . .
Pull up a folding chair!

There's a cushion 'neath the table—
If you move that tray of bedding—
Oh! The dog's been out here all day long—
So just watch where you are treading!

There's a path of concrete slabs
Running all around the lawn—
And a pond there in the corner
Just heaving with Frogspawn!

I've got an old iron bedstead
Up against the garage wall—
It was meant for climbing roses, but—
They don't seem to like it at all!

There's a rather rusty archway
With a purple Clem-a-tis!
I try to prune it every spring—
But it's rather 'hit and miss'!

The slugs have eaten the lettuce—
The tomatoes got the blight—
The moles have dug up half the lawn—
It's not a pretty sight!

My garden's not a bit like Kew—
But I'm very fond of it . . .
Though if Monty Don or Titchmarsh called . . .
I think they'd have a fit!

The Big Chill

When I was young and unaware,
I faced the snow without a care.
The chill of winter caused no pain—
I never 'dreamed' of Sunny Spain!

Now, numbness grips my fingers
And the warmth never reaches my toes.
My ears—they sting in the cold winter wind
And icicles hang from my nose!

There's frost on the kitchen window
And the butter's too hard to spread.
The hot porridge just makes my nose run,
So I think I'll go back to bed!

The thermostat has gone awry.
My feet are still cold, though it's way up high!
No, it's not much fun now I'm wrinkly and old—
'Cos I don't half feel the bloomin' cold!

Control!

There's a gremlin deep inside me
Who keeps trying to get out.
I have to keep him locked away—
Of that there is no doubt!

For every time he surfaces
And I let him have his way
His gluttony is awesome—
He eats and eats all day!

He reaches for the chocolate,
Cream cakes and apple pie;
He quite ignores the healthy food
I normally keep by!

I really can't control him,
And his greed just makes me groan . . .
'Cos when I jump upon the scales . . .
I've put on half a stone!

Enough!

I cleared out Grandad's wardrobe today
And there to my surprise
I found ten long-sleeved sweatshirts
And twenty assorted ties!
There were shoes only fit for the dustbin
And nineteen pairs of socks
Then eight belts in different sizes,
So I put them all in a box!

Two blazers with bright silver buttons,
Four white shirts and a suit that's too small;
Another ten short-sleeved summer shirts
And a waistcoat he won't wear at all!
Six pairs of grey flannel trousers . . .
And his underwear drawers are packed tight;
Four unopened packs of handkerchiefs
All waiting to see the light!

So, please DON'T give him clothes on his birthday,
For his wardrobe is totally stuffed—
Go back to the Liquorice ALLSORTS 'cos—
ENOUGH IS ENOUGH IS ENOUGH!

The Early Bird!

I've hardened off the Hollyhocks;
Summer's on its way!
I've fertilized the Fuchsias—
(It's very nearly May!)

I've weeded all the Wallflowers—
They're quite a sight to see!
I've tied up the Tomatoes . . .
And sprayed the Apple Tree!

I've power-sprayed the Patio
And overhauled the mower;
I've pruned the Pelargoniums—
Can't wait for them to flower!

I've raked all through the Roses
And spread the horse's dung;
Tidied up the Troughs and Tubs
And the baskets are all hung!

I've bedded the Begonias
And the Lawn has been de-mossed—
I've mulched around the Marrows . . .
And NOW . . .
they've forecast . . .
FROST?!

Familiar Faces!

Now I'm sure I've seen that face before . . .
She really looks familiar . . .
Was she my uncle Joe's first wife?
If not, she's very sim'lar!
Oh, I hope she doesn't see me;
Now, whatever was she called?
I think it began with W . . .
Oh, good grief—she's nearly bald!

I'll pretend I haven't seen her . . .
Now what price is this tin of Peas?
Oh, no! She's heading straight for me . . .
Think now! What *is* her name . . . Please!

'Oh, hello! How lovely to see you!
My goodness, how long has it been?
No, you haven't changed a bit either—
Despite the years between!
And how's the family keeping?'
(Come on now—please give me a clue!)
Oh, why don't I have the courage to say . . .
'Just who the dickens are you?'

The Vulgarity of the Common Cold!

A Cold is very common . . .
It doesn't give a fig . . .
Whether you're just a petty thief—
Or a High-Court Judge in a wig!

A Cold is – oh - so common . . .
In fact, it's quite uncouth!
Though it never really bothered me much . . .
When I was in my youth!

A Cold is terribly vulgar . . .
And it's so much worse when you're old . . .
It's rude and mean and quite obscene . . .
I cough and sneeze—it's most unclean . . .
I really should be in quarantine . . .
It's a miserable thing—is a Cold!

Wasp Wa(i)sted!

There are a lot of things in this old life
That really are not fair . . .
Like the lottery being won <u>again</u>
By a multi-millionaire!
Or a skinny girl in a mere size eight,
Who sits down for a meal and piles her plate
With chips and pasties and Mayo to boot . . .
While my greatest treat is a piece of fruit!
I confess I have a sweet tooth . . .
For sugar and chocolate I crave . . .
But I have to eat salad and chicken and sprouts . . .
For the calories I must save!

Now, the wasp, he has a sweet tooth,
So why is his waist so thin?
And he doesn't need a corset
To hold his stomach in!
Did ever you see a fat wasp . . .
All breathless and waddling around . . .
And so full of puddings and chocolate,
That he hardly could get off the ground?
You watch him at a picnic . . .
When you spread the blanket out,
He and his mates are all waiting . . .
Circling in droves round about!
And he never goes for sandwiches—
Unless they're full up with jam . . .
He won't even look at the salmon
Or your slices of chicken and ham!

No! He always makes a bee-line
For the ice cream and lemon curd tart!
He leaves all the cheese and the salad
And health food that's good for your heart!

Now and then, though, if he's not looking . . .
And in treacle he's up to his knees . . .
(And, oh, so caref'ly avoiding
That slice of low fat cheese!)
You can stop his wee caper . . .
With a rolled-up newspaper . . .
And his black-hearted bingeing will cease . . .
While you finish your picnic in Peace!

Why?

Oh, why can't I be like Twiggy?
All beautifully lithe and slim . . .
I wonder if she has to diet . . .
Or spend hours in a boring old gym!

Oh, why can't I be like Twiggy
Look great in whatever I wear . . .
With such fabulous clothes in my wardrobe . . .
And a stylist to see to my hair!

So—why can't I be like Twiggy!
She's nearly as old as I . . .
Yet her skin is so smooth and she looks so young . . .
While I'm wrinkly and fat—tell me, 'WHY!'

Final Plea (or Pee!)

Now I know we all have to go sometime . . .
So I'm putting this up on my 'Blog' . . .
'Cos I just have this dread . . .
And it has to be said . . .
I just don't want to die on the 'bog'!

I've a tendency t'ward constipation . . .
And in order to just do a 'poo' . . .
It's a strain on my heart . . .
But joking apart . . .
Please don't let me die on the 'loo'!

Oh, please let me die with my clothes on . . .
Though I don't like to lower the tone . . .
If my bottom's exposed . . .
Keep the bathroom door closed . . . Make sure
nobody sees . . . But most of all PLEASE . . .
Just don't let me die on the 'throne'!

Things Ain't What They Used to Be

I know not why, in years gone by . . .
The days were always sunny . . .
When cigarettes were fashionable
And comedians—they were funny!

Back then, 'Coke' was kept in the Coalhouse!
And 'Grass'—well, grass was just mown!
A 'Weed' was dug out with a garden hoe . . .
And a 'Joint' was Roast Beef on the Bone!

Dishwashers worked hard for a paltry wage . . .
Tumble-driers had not been invented . . .
Our wallets weren't bulging with credit cards;
You got paid every week and you spent it!

DVDs and CDs and Nintendo WIs;
Computers and Mice and IT . . .
Docking Stations and mem'ry sticks MP3s
It's Gobblegook to me!

Take me back to the days before Duvets . . .
When the sheets were crisp and white . . .
Before Quilts became Continental . . .
And Blankets were tucked in tight!

'In Town Tonight' on a Saturday night . . .
Scrumping apples from Uncle Bert's tree . . .
Fish and chips wrapped in yesterday's papers . . .
Things ain't what they used to be!

Hide and Seek!

Have you seen my car keys, Bill?
They're not on the usual hook—
I'm due at the Doctors at half-past ten
And I'm late now, so please help me look!

Now what did I do with my glasses, Bill?
I had them a minute ago—
They must be around here somewhere;
It's only a bungalow!

And where did I put those scissors, Bill?
I had them just yesterday!
I've searched and searched all over the place—
I was sure that I'd put them away.

Now where did I leave my gloves, Bill,
'Cos it's really quite cold outside?
Oh, why do I spend so many long hours . . .
Searching so far and so wide?

Do we share this house with a Gremlin,
Whose mission in life is to hide
All the things that I need—
Though I must concede . . .
I should strive every day
to put thing away . . .
In their rightful place . . .
And I know that's the case . . .
But my brain's 'gone to pot' . . .
And my eyesight is 'shot' . . .
It's a PROBLEM that can't be denied!

Arachnophobia!

It's surely not his size that frightens me . . .
He's really very small!
It's not the way he stares at me and waits . . .
I must seem very tall!
I watch in fear and trembling—
Not knowing where he'll run . . .
It makes no sense at all!

They tell me a spider will do lots of good . . .
If a dirty fly he ensnares!
They say that he's much more frightened of me . . .
But it's *me* that he always scares!
And I'm filled with dread by those long gangly legs . . .
Festooned with 'tickly' hairs!

He stands quite still and fixes me,
With his 'evil spider' stare . . .
Then swiftly scuttles off towards . . .
The darkness of his lair . . .
And I become a 'witless nervous wreck'—
Irrational beyond repair!

Chaos in the Cabbage Patch
(or Bedlam in the Borders!)

I'm glad I'm not a garden snail . . .
That leaves a slimy, mucous trail . . .
Without his shell, he's incredibly frail,
If a hungry thrush gets hold of his tail
. . . He makes a tasty SNACK!

I'm glad I'm not a Vine-weevil . . .
'Cos EVERYONE thinks that he's evil!
And his offspring consider it gleeful . . .
To chomp through the roots—which is lethal
. . . If he were a sheep, he'd be BLACK!

I'm glad I'm not a furry Mole—
With velvet coat as black as coal,
Who's always in trouble for digging his hole . . .
Right under the lawn . . . the poor little soul
. . . Takes an awful lot of <u>FLAK</u> !!

I'm glad I'm not a slimy slug . . .
A persecuted garden thug . . .
Or any other kind of bug,
That lurks beneath the wooden trug
. . . Or hides in a hessian *SACK*!

No – I'm glad I'm not one of those garden pests,
That hides in the shade of the undergrowth – lest . . .
The Gard'ner comes round and finds out they've
transgressed . . .
And no matter how loudly they might protest . . .
He dispatches them all with a *THWACK*!

Power Games

She sits, resigned . . . Most every night,
While he decides what to view . . .
He browses through the TV Times . . .
It's a question of 'power'—Nothing new!
He flicks from side . . . to side . . . to side . . .
With sport as his ultimate goal!
He rules the roost from his fireside chair . . .
The King of Remote Control!

And there she sits, without complaint,
As her nightly vigil she keeps . . .
Soon his tired eyes will start to close . . .
And then he'll drift off to sleep!
He loosens his grip on the 'trophy' . . .
She removes it with a wry smile!
She reigns triumphant—Queen at last . . .
At least for a little while!

No more Darts, Top Gear or the Cricket,
No more War Films or Match of the Day!
With a flick of the switch, she turns over—
Now it's 'Strictly' and 'Home and Away!'

Twixt Me and You

My 'bits and bobs' are wearing out
. . . it's True!
My 'get up and go' has long since gone
. . . it Flew!
Right out the door in search of
. . .pastures New!
My teeth are rather far between . . .
. . . and Few!
I have to be selective of the things . . .
. . . I Chew!
My hips are held in place by just . . .
. . . a Screw!
I daren't bend down to buckle up . . .
. . . my Shoe!
And though it's strictly just twixt me . . .
. . . and You!
I sometimes barely make it to . . .
. . . the Loo!
(It's a worry when you're waiting in . . .
. . . a Queue!)
Meeting people in the street that I . . .
. . . once Knew!
I stand there wond'ring who I'm
. . .talking To!
It's a nightmare when you just don't have
. . . a Clue!

But it happens to us all . . . it's
. . . nothing New!
And I try to take an . . .
. . . optimistic View!
So when people stop and ask, 'How do . . .
. . . you do!'
I smile a toothless smile—'I'm fine . . .
. . .and You!'

'Hair' Today and 'Blonde' Tomorrow!

I've been straightened; I've been crimped;
I've been permanently waved . . .
I've had 'pageboys'; I've had 'beehives'
And I've been completely shaved!

I've been black, and I've been yellow;
I've been red, and I've been blue . . .
I've been green and brown and ginger
With a streak of purple, too!

But, now I'm in my dotage . . .
(That's the years 'they' call twilight!)
I think my hair deserves a rest,
From being quite so bright!

So—it's just 'shampoo and blow-dry' . . .
Not a chemical in sight!
'Cos in spite of all that colouring . . .
My hair's completely WHITE!

THE END

A Short Autobiography
of the Author

I was born, Helen Middleton, in Oxford in England, in January 1936 and spent 4 years during the second world war as an evacuee in America, at St. Pauls School in Concord, New Hampshire, at the home of Henry Kittredge, who was, at that time, the English master.

On my return to Oxford in late 1944, I was educated at St. Juliana's Convent and, after moving down to Hampshire with my family, I attended South Wilts Grammar School in Salisbury.

At the age of 16, I met, and later married, Bill, with whom I was to spend the next sixty, happy years, until he died in 2012. We spent a large part of our lives watching, and playing, cricket and raising four wonderful children, who have since extended our family with 10 grandchildren and (to date) 5 great-grandchildren, who are all equally wonderful.

In my seventies, I joined a local Creative Writing Class and, being rather lazy, found it much more fun to write poetry and even more fun when my poems made people smile!!"

Lightning Source UK Ltd.
Milton Keynes UK
UKOW03f2356060417

298528UK00002B/149/P

9 781524 595067